Social Net Effect:
Fishing For Prospects
With Social Media
Marketing

MICHEAL J. SAVOIE

ISBN: 1499715641
ISBN-13: 978-1499715644

DEDICATION

I dedicate this book first and foremost to the friends and fans I have met
on each of the social media platforms I covered in this book. Without your
attention, nothing else would have been possible.
Also, to Ken McArthur, without whom I would not have been exposed to
the dream of using social media to get in front of millions of eyeballs in a
very short amount of time.
And finally, to Yvonne, who has given me the motivation to excel at
everything I do – I love you!

CONTENTS

ACKNOWLEDGMENTS

I want to acknowledge my mentor, Ross Goldberg, for hanging in with me when it seemed like I was lost. The traffic training I received from you really made a difference.
I also wish to acknowledge Victor Nyorani, who did the majority of the research on this book.

A WORD FROM MICHEAL

Social media marketing is the dissemination of your company's brand (if your company has planned out its marketing strategy that far) into the online world through the use of social networks. While that definition opens up a whole lot of new questions, it is the mission of this book to reveal to the small business owner how to start a successful social media marketing strategy without investing a lot of time and money.

That is not to say that it will not cost either time or money. Social media marketing requires research, planning and effort. Without these, the business owner is going to make mistakes that could set the business back or at the very least not impact the business at all. The research is necessary to find the right audience for the marketing. The planning is necessary to design a brand for uniformity of message. Finally, without effort, the social media marketing strategies will die on the vine.

If you do not have the time to invest in your social media campaigns, you may have to outsource to people who are trained to do social media marketing for you. This will cost money, but the time savings are enormous.

Social networks have arisen out of the fibers of the World Wide Web, and each network is a small hub of interactivity for millions of people. As I cover some of the recommended networks in the following chapters, remember that you do not have to work all of them at the same time right away. Each one has strengths and weaknesses that will become evident as I go through them. They will still be important for you to target, but you will have to work them into your marketing mix gradually if you do not have a team helping you.

First and foremost, before any social media marketing campaign, your business needs to have a central hub. A place where your marketing message is intermingled with information for interested parties. It is alright to have a page that talks about your company's accomplishments and accolades, but your site's main focus should be on helping a potential customer into your marketing funnel.

I use website and blog interchangeably in this book, but I highly recommend that your website be a blog. A blog has ceased being an online journal and blossomed into a content management system capable of serving up sales pages, shopping carts and frequently asked questions (FAQ) pages to help move potential customers closer to the buying decision. So when I talk about a blog, think corporate website.

When you plan your brand (or your marketing - if you do not feel you need to brand your business) message - the first place it should become evident is on your blog. The color schemes, the photos and banners should reflect your marketing brand. When a marketing message is not uniform across platforms, a disconnect will occur in your prospect, and you could lose them before they take the next step.

By connecting your blog to the various social media platforms discussed in this book, you will be forming the strands of your Social Net. This net is one you will be using to fish for prospects that are looking for your solution to their pain. The way this works is what I call the Social Net Effect.

INTRODUCTION

The online world offers an unprecedented variety of platforms through which to market your business, source for clients and sell merchandise or services. Millions of blogs, websites and especially social sites are readily available as prime marketing platforms. However, this wide variety of choices can create one of two scenarios:

Case 1: An often witnessed scenario in many marketing strategies presents a woefully uncoordinated and incompatible patchwork of branding and marketing efforts, spread out across different online platforms. This usually occurs when a marketing team is overwhelmed by the diversity of choice and lacks a coordinated and well-designed strategy. What you end up with is a disappointed clientele, confused by the lack of uniformity and inconsistency of your marketing efforts on the various platforms.

In such a scenario, it is not unusual to find clients exclaiming, "I saw an offer by company X on Facebook, but am not really sure whether it is genuine, since there is not much information about it on their website." As a result, the worst that can happen is your target audience simply ignores you, because they just don't get your message.

Case 2: Have you ever read a post on Facebook or Twitter and you were completely sure who posted it; even without checking who did? Alternatively, you might have realized that you can hardly go through a day without noting the presence of certain brands on Facebook, Twitter, LinkedIn or Instagram – either from their posts or through online friends. Moreover, when you transition from the social platform to their blogs or websites, you don't feel as if you're moving from one company to a totally different one.

Such visibility and consistency in branding develops confidence and trust in many internet users who are sure to turn into long term clients. This can only be achieved by applying the "Social Net Effect" to your business's social media branding and marketing strategy.

The Social Net Effect

Many business owners and professionals do not realize the significance of every single post, comment, photo tag or like that they make in social media. It may just take a seemingly insignificant rant about a meaningless issue to turn off a potential client. Therefore, every action taken in social media must deliberately and consistently reflect the brand of your business. Although many people in social media are prone to reckless and unprofessional behavior, you must never be one of them.

Furthermore, it's never enough to just make a few posts on Facebook and Twitter hoping that someone will take note. Social media requires a completely different set of skills compared to blogging which gets a lot of traffic simply from organic keyword search. With social media, you must aggressively deploy an abundance of posts and comments so as to get as much attention as possible.

The process of deploying abundant and consistently professional content in social media is similar to what a fisherman would do by spreading out a strong and expansive net into the sea – any small, weak net will just not do. Each strand of the fisherman's net represents every single post or comment that you make in social media. Hence, all posts must be uniformly representative of the strong values of your business in order to draw potential clients to your company's sales page. Otherwise, any weaknesses in your "net" will simply let the "fish" through.

By applying the "Social Net Effect", you will have a highly visible social media presence that strongly delivers the business brand – guaranteed to draw in many clients to your company's sales page.

How To Execute The Social Net Effect

Perhaps, you are thinking, "This Social Net Effect sounds quite good, but it might require too much time (which I do not have) and financial resources (which I also do not have)". Well, that is the reason for writing this book. Through it, you will learn highly efficient strategies to get the much-needed visibility and strong brand recognition in social media.

To develop a powerful Social Net Effect, you need to first develop a strong and highly effective brand. This is the brand that you will deploy in the select social media platforms. You must also constantly apply the actions that deliver highest returns to ensure long term success. This book details the process from beginning to end, giving the most efficient and effective strategies to use.

BRANDING YOURSELF FOR MAXIMUM EFFECT

Why are only a select few out of the thousands of brands remembered consistently? The reason is incredibly simple, but many professionals and business owners take it for granted. Most of them try to create an outward impression of who they are or what their business represents, yet such supposed characteristics do not exist internally. If you present yourself as an expert in a particular field, your expert credentials would be put to the test, especially in the highly inquisitive social media world. Therefore, your personal or company brand must originate from within.

Your brand must also flow seamlessly and uniformly throughout all online platforms. This includes blogs, websites as well as social media. This aspect is especially critical if you wish to derive the exponential benefits of the Social Net Effect in your social media marketing strategy. The reason being that all content you post in social platforms is intended to draw clients to your business sales page through links. If someone follows a link provided in your Facebook page only to end up on a website presenting a completely different impression of your company - he or she will think twice before buying from you. For instance, if you claim to be an expert in all aspects of building renovation and maintenance within your Facebook page, yet your website only contains plumbing solutions, you are bound to lose many clients who click through your links.

Branding within social media also presents a whole set of challenges completely different from traditional media. This is because your brand is only good enough when given a seal of approval by the target audience. Hence there are two steps you should take in branding yourself for maximum effect on social media – that is if you are not branding just for the sake of branding.

Step One: Develop A Truthful Brand

When developing a personal or company brand, you must be truthful to yourself as well as your target audience. Being truthful to yourself is particularly useful in personal branding (the persona you present in your profiles on social media). In this case, you must admit to yourself why you do what you do, especially since so many activities that people engage in are purely for the sake of monetary gain.

When developing a personal brand in social media, never confuse your true passion with something that you like doing because it pays your bills. People want to associate with the real you – not the entrepreneur you or business owner you or employee you. You must be completely frank with yourself; otherwise your false mask will be rudely unveiled by the very people you seek to please. A business image is better suited on a Facebook fan page rather than a profile.

Developing a company brand, on the other hand, stems from what you can do. Hence, you need to be completely honest to your target audience about what you can actually do. In fact, people are willing to recognize you as the best carpenter ever (if that is what you are good at), but will write you off completely if you claim to be a consultant in real estate development for which you have no credentials.

Once you understand where your passion lies and also what you can and cannot do, developing a unique and outstanding brand becomes easier. The combination of your individual talents and your business offering can make a powerful and unique brand for your business. In fact, some of the biggest and most recognizable personalities in business have actually used this combination to maximum effect. Such people as Sir Richard Branson, Founder of Virgin Atlantic come to mind. His adventurous and highly experimental persona has been so intertwined with his business ventures that you can hardly separate one from the other. This has made his business brand not only unique, but very memorable.

After having developed a business brand, traditional branding strategies normally head straight towards deploying adverts on social platforms. Doing this is a sure disaster in social media. To be successful on this platform, you must always involve your target audience in the actions you take. Hence, the branding process must necessarily involve your fans and friends in social media.

Step Two: Involve Social Media Audience In The Branding Process

Have you ever imagined having people work for your company, but expecting nothing in return except the sheer excitement it brings? Well, with social media that is not only possible, but many creative companies have effectively deployed such a strategy in their branding process and marketing campaigns.

Social media is a unique platform where people develop a sense of belonging to something that they get fully involved in. Therefore, if you want people to develop an attachment to your brand, they must be involved in creating it – at least to some extent. The trick is creating a situation in which your branding process will involve your fans coming in to do what they enjoy.

An excellent example of this is the Coca-Cola Super Bowl commercial that involved participation of their fans. The "Coke Chase" 2013 campaign was modeled as a competition involving three teams (Showgirls, Cowboys and Bad Landers). Coca-Cola Facebook fans determined the outcome of the competition by voting in. This pulled in the participation of thousands of fans. Such a strategy is far removed from the traditional model of putting up adverts which your audience has no part to play in (except maybe to buy something).

By involving your fans in telling the story of your brand, they not only feel a sense of attachment to it, but they can also turn into paying customers. This strategy is highly efficient and effective in delivering returns for the business.

The way to apply this engaging process can be as radical and creative as you can imagine. In fact, it must be uniquely different from other strategies; otherwise it will not have enough excitement and attraction to draw in many fans.

☐

TOP SOCIAL PLATFORMS YOU MUST BE USING

Experienced fishermen will advise you never to lay your bait in just one area – the wider you cast your net, the better the catch. This definitely applies when selecting various social platforms to enhance the overall Social Net Effect. By spreading your influence and visibility across different social sites, you not only increase your chances of getting more clients, but also build your credibility as a strong brand worth taking note of.

Another great benefit of using various social platforms is the chance to present the same message in different styles suited to each social site. Such social sites as Twitter and Facebook have a much more casual atmosphere as compared to the more professional demeanor of LinkedIn. This also gives you the chance to communicate messages in one site that would be inappropriate in another site. In this instance, casual or fun messages would be more appropriately used on Facebook or Instagram, rather than LinkedIn.

Twitter

Twitter presents an excellent platform for a casual yet intelligent conversation. Indeed, many real life movements and social upheavals have been spurred on through this platform. If used decisively, it can generate great interest in your brand guaranteed to turn into tangible benefits for your company. However, there are some basic guidelines to follow in order to get the benefits of this social site.

Show Your Personality

This is where a combination of your personal traits and business brand is necessary. Tweets that sound as if they were posted by an unfeeling robot can hardly spur such emotive debates as those loaded with sarcasm, fun or empathy. A social media marketer has to always remember that on the other side of the computer screen are human beings with feelings and emotions. Having this in mind will help in keeping your tweets human rather than robotic.

You must also gauge the feelings of your audience and anticipate the emotions that your tweets are likely to cause in them. By doing this, you will avert many disastrous outcomes caused by tactless tweeting on highly emotive issues.

Avoid Over-tweeting

The issue of over-tweeting should not be a concern if you spread your "net" across various social platforms. In the intervals that you are not tweeting, you could be posting on Facebook, LinkedIn, Pinterest or Instagram. This means that your presence will be continually felt in the social media world without over-exposure on any one social site.

Why is over-tweeting bad? Simply because nobody wants to have a conversation with someone who talks all the time, but gives you no time to respond. You don't really want to turn twitter into a personal blog or impersonal website. By giving your audience enough time to respond to your tweets, you will build a rapport through meaningful interaction.

Always Reply Promptly

The term social media has conversation and interaction as its core agenda. Hence, if you rarely reply to people's comments or tweets, you stand out as a wolf among sheep. When your followers notice this, they usually give your "dead" tweets a wide berth.

By replying to tweets, you build an understanding relationship with many potential clients who sometimes just need the assurance that you are a real human on the other side – not a robot. Giving prompt replies is also one sign of a business that values its clients. This is an essential factor for any service-centered business.

Facebook

The power of Facebook is not only its enormous reach, but also the facilities on offer to effectively make your Facebook numbers count. This platform is perhaps the most business-friendly social site compared to all the rest (explained in greater detail in chapter four of this book).

Just as with Twitter, you must always have a back and forth interaction with your Facebook friends or fans and also avoid "rabid" posting. However, the issue of personality has a different twist in Facebook as well as other unique characteristics.

Keep Your Facebook Profile Personal And Fan Page Professional

A big mistake that many people make on Facebook fan pages is letting their personalities get the better of them. You should always maintain your business brand image in Facebook fan pages even when posting casual and fun stuff. If you really have to let off some steam, the best place to do so would be your Facebook profile (at least your friends will understand).

Facebookers clearly understand the difference between a fan page and a profile. In case posts in your fan page get out of character, the expectations of your fans would be betrayed. When this happens, Facebook fans would seriously question the inappropriateness of posts on relationships within a comedy fan page, for instance. Doing so once in a while may be forgiven, but making it a habit will critically affect the participation of fans.

Spam Not!

Many incidents of spamming on Facebook go unnoticed due to the largely forgiving, friendly environment. However, if you send repeated Facebook page invitations to friends, you are likely to get blocked by them. By blocking you, they will not get any updates of your posts or even comments.

Maintain Facebook etiquette that involves respecting other Facebookers' privacy even if they never complain about intrusions. Facebook is a closely intimate social platform, but there is always a limit to how close you can get to anyone.

Instagram

The online world is more receptive to visual cues than anything else. When people see you, they tend to feel as if they already know you. In fact, it is not uncommon for popular personalities to be stopped on the streets by excited fans simply because they "know them" (read: they have seen the celebrity on TV). Therefore, the social media marketing strategy of your business must make maximum use of the Instagram photo sharing facility.

By following a few basic guidelines, this is guaranteed to constantly keep you in sight of your target audience.

Not All About You

When you put up photos that include people unrelated to your business, you are not losing the spotlight. In fact, you are actually gaining by portraying yourself as a people-person. Even if the main intention of posting photos is to display your talents, skills and accomplishments; you must always include other people in some photos. If not, you will appear as the only lonely person within an interactive social platform.

Tell A Story

Any skilled photographer can take a photo and share it on Instagram. Hence, it is only the unique story behind your photos that will draw in crowds. This means finding creative ways to add your unique personality to the images you put up. This can be done by making use of the available filters so as to convert ordinary images into works of art – or at least something interesting.

LinkedIn

You are in business, but have not joined LinkedIn – what are you waiting for? This is the perfect hangout for many professionals and businessmen. If your business provides B2B services, LinkedIn offers the best platform to present your sales pitch in a subtle and powerful way. You are also guaranteed to develop valuable networks in your profession or even meet with significant people that will give you the big break to become a rock star in social media (you can learn how to become a rock star in chapter eight of this book).

Honesty Is Key

With other social platforms, you could easily fool many fans that you are an expert in a certain field. That can hardly pass in LinkedIn. The highly acclaimed and qualified professionals on this platform are sure to put you to the test. You definitely do not want to come off looking as a fraud.

Presenting your true credentials is the first step to getting the most useful network in your profession or business. By doing this, you can associate with similarly qualified individuals through whom you will learn how to handle the challenges that you face.

Only Endorse People You Know

In Twitter, you could follow someone with the hope that such a person would follow you back. However, endorsing a complete stranger in LinkedIn in exchange for a similar endorsement can be disastrous for your brand image. What if it turns out that you have endorsed a quack doctor? Worse still, your clients may take confidence in the person simply because of your endorsement.

Pinterest

Pinterest in the social media world is getting bigger each passing day, and is by all indications here to stay. Any business owner that wants to be successful in their niche market understands the importance of leveraging social media for lead generation. Pinterest is fast becoming a favorite for many businesses today starting from small businesses to the large corporations. When all is said and done, Pinterest simply cannot be ignored. To understand the real power of Pinterest lead generation, it is important to take a look at two companies that can be deemed to be model examples.

Case Study 1 – Perpetual Kid

Perpetual Kid, which is an online store selling entertainment products for children, is one such example. The company began their Pinterest marketing campaign in earnest in the summer of 2011, and the exposure has been great for the company to say the least. At the beginning of their Pinterest marketing campaign, the social media site was responsible for only 0.20% of the Company's total traffic. By the beginning of 2012 (January), the number had risen to 2.63%. According to Perpetual Kid, Pinterest leads are twice as likely to convert into actual sales as compared to Facebook and other social media sites.

Case Study 2 - Wayfair

Another good example to look at is one of the largest home goods retailers, Wayfair. According to the company's CEO Niraj Shah, leads generated by Pinterest were 10% more likely to convert into actual sales as compared to other social media sites, including Twitter and Facebook. She also confesses that Pinterest customers on average spend 10% more on products than customers who arrive from other social media platforms. The CEO further reveals that the visual imagery on Pinterest is the single most important factor that makes people want to buy products.

FACEBOOK: PROFILE OR FAN PAGE?

The launch of Facebook fan pages in 2007 presented a golden opportunity for countless professionals and businessmen to showcase their skills, products and services to a much wider audience than was possible with a Facebook profile. Any businessman or professional who is not taking advantage of this great facility is missing out on a powerful opportunity to cast his "net" further into the social world.

To appreciate the significance of a Facebook fan page as a powerful social media marketing tool, you first have to know the limitations of a Facebook profile.

Facebook Profile

A Facebook profile represents your persona on this social platform. It is ideally the place where you establish your personal brand – a useful aspect for public figures and professionals. The aspect of personal branding and ability to send unlimited private messages to all Facebook friends are the major benefits of a Facebook profile. Unfortunately, a profile is limited to a maximum of only 5,000 friends which is a major drawback to your efforts at reaching as many people as possible. Moreover, using a personal profile to market a business would greatly affect the credibility of your business. That is simply out of the question.

Facebook Fan Page

This option offers many useful facilities that can greatly enhance your marketing efforts in social media. It has various key aspects that are beneficial to any social media marketing campaign.

Managed By Administrators

You can ensure that your Facebook fan page has uninterrupted 24-hour activity simply by appointing a regular shift of administrators. Indeed, several companies have used their fan pages as customer service centers, where client queries are handled by administrators at any time of day.

Having a good number of administrators gives the posts of the page a wider reach, since the posts appear in the news feeds of administrators' profiles. This can help in maximizing the reach of a Facebook fan page without using targeted ads.

Insight Data

Data is vital to the success of any business. It is what tells you whether you are winning or losing; otherwise, you are simply playing a game of chance. Facebook fan pages are designed to cater to the needs of business brands by offering a wide array of information concerning: fan demographics; reach of your posts and fan page activity among others. This will help you identify the high impact areas so that you can focus on them.

Added Functionality With Apps

To maximize on the Social Net Effect, use of Facebook apps is a must in your social media marketing strategy. Basically, fan pages already have custom functionalities, but many other third party apps are useful for specific purposes. Such apps include customer apps for gathering email leads for marketing purposes outside Facebook. This is immensely beneficial, since the more contacts you have of potential clients, the more opportunities there are of interacting with them. In the process of such interaction, many clients make buying decisions.

Hyper-Targeted Ads

Although it is always preferable to draw in fans organically (especially in the initial stages), hyper-targeted ads can give your page the much needed boost in numbers. Only make sure that you have meaningful content that your target audience would want. Facebook makes your advertising work easier by giving you a variety of demographics from which to select your target audience. You can target specific age groups, certain geographical locations or other important aspects.

Post Scheduling

The post scheduling facility available in Facebook fan pages allows you to plan your posting content ahead of time. This is useful in marketing efforts, whereby you can synchronize particular posts to coincide with various business timetables. If you intend to have a sale, for instance, you can set the tone and prepare your fans in advance for the future occurrence (you can read more on planning content in chapter 6 of this book). Having a pre-planned content strategy will give you more time to focus on other critical business activities.

Creative Ways Of Using A Fan Page

The content in Fan page does not always have to come from administrators. Your fans can play a useful role in producing interesting content for you. This not only increases interaction with fans, but also gives the page posts a much wider reach.

A good example of this can be seen in the Firehouse Subs Facebook page. Customers were offered free prizes simply for snapping pictures with NASCAR driver cutouts found in the Firehouse Sub restaurants. These images were then used as content on the fan page. Having their images on the Firehouse Sub fan page encouraged many customers to create a buzz about the page as they shared with friends. The result is a greater impact and wider reach of the page even without too much effort in developing content.

TWITTER: HOW TO TWEET SO THEY WILL HEAR YOU!

The hard truth is no matter how great your tweets are, they will never amount to much if you only have a few hundred followers. Simple logic shows that the more people you reach, the higher your chances of netting in paying clients for your business through social media. Therefore, this means that you must first get a large following even before thinking about being heard.

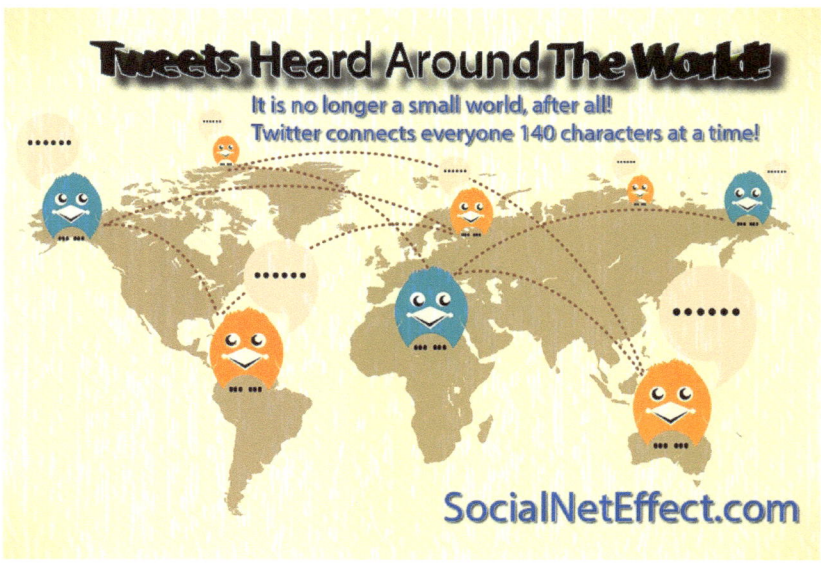

Perhaps, people are also not listening to you simply because you have such a small following – most people get attracted to accounts that have large following. In fact, just that label of having a large following makes people stop and listen. Hence, getting attention should be the very first step. Thereafter, you need to take advantage of the opportunities readily available at your disposal to get everybody listening.

Step One: Get Their Attention

If you have any experience on social platforms, you would realize that no one will ever connect with you if they have no idea that you exist (maybe just one or two highly inquisitive people who might be marketing agents just like you).

In order to get the initial attention, you must start by following as many accounts as possible. Try to focus on people who you think will be most interested in what you have to offer. Such people will give you the best start to your Twitter account. Your main intention in following others is for them to follow you back. A few will follow you back. However, a majority of them will need a bit more motivation to do so.

The next move to take is tweeting on topics that impact directly on the issues concerning those you have followed. This will require you to follow up on the questions they ask and what they talk about. With a bit of research, you can come up with useful information regarding many issues. By doing this, you present yourself as being selfless rather than simply interested in getting many followers. People will take note and soon you will start building up a good following by applying this strategy consistently.

Step Two: Find The Best Time To Tweet

Just as with many other aspects in life, Twitter has its most active and inactive times. You might have to re-organize your personal or business schedule to fit in with these Twitter periods. For instance, if most of your Twitter followers are active in the evening, schedule your social media activity to this time. The morning and afternoon periods may be used for other business activities.

The activity on Twitter varies from country to country and also depends on the specific demographic of Twitter users. Working class people would be more active during the evenings – after working hours. If this group of people is your target audience, then you have to schedule more tweets during the evening.

Step Three: Bring In Your Email Subscribers

Having varied online platforms for marketing your business is beneficial since one platform can easily complement another. For instance, your company website can provide a good source of twitter followers out of the website's mail newsletter subscribers.

Email subscribers are already willing to listens to what you have to say – that's why they subscribed to your website' newsletter anyway. After inviting them through email, this group is likely to be your most ardent listeners on Twitter. They also have a high regard for your expertise, hence the will not be too hard to please.

Step Four: Become A Fun-filled Wikipedia

No one wants to hang out with a know-it-all who never misses the opportunity to show how much he knows. On the other hand, everyone will be more than glad to have an intelligent friend who knows how to have some fun. The choice is up to you: whether you want to be the former or the latter. Hint: the latter is way better.

When tweeting, you need to present your expert opinion, but never put out dry and complex sounding tweets that look like text book material. When you present well informed tweets, your followers will listen and by making it fun and interesting, they will love you for it. Many clients like to see the human side of companies on social media.

Step Five: Use Conversational Tweets

Conversational tweets push the listener to react. It can either be a question; a sentence left hanging or even your perspective on a highly contentious topic that cannot go without a response.

Whenever you do ask questions, make sure that it concerns issues that your followers are really concerned about. The worst thing that can happen is ending up with an unanswered question. The people that you are asking questions should also be free enough with you to give honest answers. Hence, before asking questions, you can test the responsiveness of your Twitter followers by gauging there comment on regular tweets.

PIN THE TALE ON YOUR MARKET – PINTEREST LEAD GENERATION

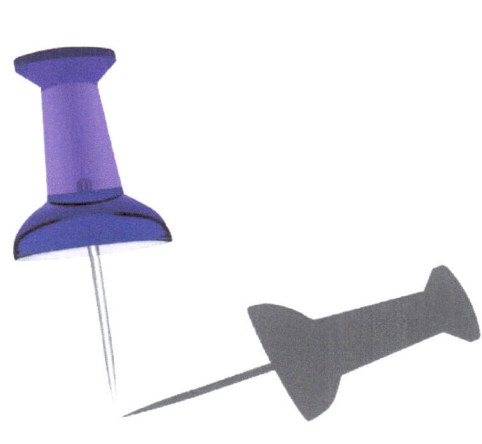

Telling a story with pictures is the whole reason for existence of Pinterest! Businesses who share photos that tell the right story, help get leads to their website. And the numbers are telling an exciting story for Pinterest.

In the past year alone, the number of unique visitors to Pinterest has grown from 700,000 to 20 Million and the numbers keep rising. It is estimated that 1 in 4 consumers are now spending less time on other social media sites in favor of Pinterest according to data made available by the Competes' Online Shopper Intelligence Survey.

It is also estimated that 25% of consumers will end up purchasing a product or service that they have seen on Pinterest. For the longest time, this social media site was deemed primarily for women shoppers, although recent statistics reveal otherwise. According to a survey by Compete, 17% of women bought a product or service that they had seen on Pinterest, while the same is true for 37% of their male counterparts. All these are reasons for any business to take advantage of this social media platform to gain exposure and market their business. That being said, here are some

Pinterest lead generation tips that any business can use to increase the number of prospects heading back to their website.

#1: Posting Blog Images

This is an important part of leveraging Pinterest for your business. It means pinning images from your blogs with the appropriate links back to the related blog post. This is a quick and easy way for Pinterest lead generation that doesn't require too much work on your part in the long-run.

#2: Take Advantage Of Infographics

The world today is all about the visuals. This is a great opportunity for your graphic designer to come up with visually compelling data points for your company or business. This is a chance to engage Pinterest users with unique and engaging visual content that projects your business in a positive light. Again, be sure to link this back to your website to generate leads using Pinterest.

#3: Whitepaper And eBook Covers

If your business has created a whitepaper or an eBook, pinning the cover onto your business' Pinterest brand page is a good idea to capture the curiosity of your audience. The world today is fast paced and information driven; and providing useful content in the form of eBooks and whitepapers has proven very effective in gaining clients' trust. Remember to link the cover to the corresponding whitepaper or eBook, and remember to include the URL to a landing page and a call to action (CTA) for effective Pinterest lead generation. Try to include a CTA in your pins and images on your pinboard. Start using "repin this" "click here" and/or "comment below" on your pins and images to prompt your audience into some kind of action that will increase leads back to your website.

#4: Photos Of Happy Clients

Before people can decide to purchase your product or service, they first have to be sure that they are going to be happy with their investment. One of the most successful ways to gain clients' trust is to pin pictures of other happy clients. Be sure to first ask for permission before pinning any photos of your previous clients. You should also link the pinned photos to positive user reviews or case studies related to your product or service.

#5: Use Hashtags

Hashtags makes your content more search-engine friendly, and are supported by Pinterest. Create a pinboard for new products or services you are launching or for promoting your campaign. Use the same Twitter and Google+ hashtag to tag your pinboard to successfully sync your social media marketing efforts.

#6: Create A Video Gallery

A lot of businesses owners have no idea that it is possible to pin videos on Pinterest, and are losing out on great Pinterest lead generation opportunities. You can easily pin videos related to your business through the separate video tab on the homepage. Again, remember to add links back to your website to generate more leads and make conversion much easier.

#7: Measure Your Results

It is important to evaluate your return on investment (ROI) every so often to measure how successful your social media marketing campaign is. There are many analytic tools available to measure lead generation performance. It is important to use these analytics on your images and other content to find out what is working and what isn't. You can easily discern a pattern for failure or success to further streamline your social media marketing strategy.

HOW TO BE SEEN AND HEARD BY YOUR TARGET AUDIENCE

This is the point at which you must use the Social Net Effect to bring in real tangible benefits to your business; otherwise, it is all a waste of time. Unfortunately, the reality is many Facebook pages and Twitter accounts fail to convert their numbers into meaningful returns. You might have noticed that normal posts on such Facebook pages and Twitter accounts normally attract a lot of comments, shares and likes. However, when they post anything that is even mildly sales oriented, the interaction stops abruptly – no one wants to buy. Sometimes, the fans don't even click through the links leading to business sales pages. Such poor conversion rates, has a lot to do with how well a businessman presents his message to the target audience or if the businessman has a target audience at all.

In order to achieve high conversion rates, a businessman must keep in mind that the Facebook or Twitter accounts will most probably have more fans or followers than the intended audience. Therefore, at the critical moments that you intend to make a sales pitch to your target audience, your messages have to be extremely refined to suit the exact people you are targeting. If not, you will not only lose your target audience, but also offend all the rest. This usually happens when you present a vaguely sounding sales pitch, which is so general that none of your fans can figure out who you want to respond to the offer.

In order to develop a good plan to effectively reach your target audience, you must carry out an extensive background analysis and preparation before ever posting anything that is remotely sales oriented.

In Depth Analysis Of The Target Audience

Despite all the misgivings about using the private world of social media for commercial purposes, it does offer a great opportunity to examine the preferences of numerous potential clients. As long as you respect the privacy of your fans, a Facebook fan page offers the best chance to extensively examine the values, interests and preferences of your target audience. In fact, you can set up polls simply to get the views and preferences of potential clients.

An important aspect that you should take note of is the periods in which your target audience gets online. You should also be online at such times and avoid using automated posting applications during such periods. When you are present, you are better able to reply to any queries and build a rapport with them.

Apart from the demographic data provided by Facebook concerning your fans, you can even go further by conducting surveys to identify your preferred audience. This can be done through third-party apps which allow you to conveniently take the views of your fans. This will help identify various key factors such as income status, occupations, spending behavior among many others.

Share Content That Resonates With Your Target Audience

Once you know the necessary details of your target audience, you are better able to make a sales pitch that powerfully resonates with them. Also make sure to always reflect their interests in regular posts or at frequent intervals in your posts. This will ensure that as much as you are engaging with all your fans in general, the needs of your target audience are regularly catered to.

At those periods that you are driving towards a particular business offer, you should focus more on giving content that reflects the interests and preferences of your target audience. This will keep them interested and engaged in your fan page. Hence, the moment you present a business offer, you will have the right kind of people to take it.

Always ensure that the periods in which you specifically focus on your target audience are long enough to keep them interested, but short enough to avoid putting off the rest of your fans. By doing this, you will effectively convert a good number of the target audience into paying clients.

A good way to manage the type of content that you post on your fan page is by scheduling cycles of monthly or weekly categories. This keeps your posts unique and interesting and avoids over-emphasis on one particular topic. Moreover, it also helps in planning the type of content to post. The categories can be aligned with the various promotions, offers and other activities in your business. When you have content that complements the current business activities, it becomes easier to include links to your website for fans to get more information or involved in such activities.

Slinging The Hash(Tags)

Hashtags are one of the most important tools social media marketing. They allow users to easily find content by pooling similar content together. Use of the # symbol with a word or phrase (without spaces or punctuation) will be picked up automatically by Facebook, Twitter and Instagram to "tag" your content with whatever hashtag you choose. For example, I often use the hashtag #BlogTalkFootball on my @BlogTlkFootball Twitter account and Facebook Fan Page. That way, I can easily find my content and the responses of my tribe!

Hashtags can be very effective tools for helping you to build a following - here is how:

Brand specific hashtags:

These are hashtags that are linked to your brand specifically. These will be useful in monitoring the exposure and mentions of your company. It is important that you use the same hashtags across all the social media platforms you are on. Encourage your followers to use these hashtags when talking about your products. (#BlogTalkFootball, for example)

General Hashtags:

These are hashtags that are generally related to the nature of your product (for example, #car). These are useful in linking you to a tribe of similar businesses in the market. This ensures that you are seen by the right market and will increase your ability to generate leads.

Trending hashtags:

These show what is popular on Instagram, Twitter and Facebook at the moment. Monitor these to ensure that you get in on the right conversations.

FANNING THE FLAMES (FAN PAGE SUCCESS)

A successful Facebook fan page is not one that grows rapidly and amasses a large following with great engagement, but then disappears into oblivion a short while later. That can only be described as a one-hit wonder.

A successful fan page is one that constantly produces interesting content, is informative as well as engaging and continually grows in prominence from month to month and over the years. Such a page would be a great asset to any business, since longevity is a powerful attribute of sustainable long term growth and profitability.

The continuity of a fan page gives a much better chance for the business to reap the benefits of the Social Net Effect. This is particularly so, since developing beneficial relationships with potential customers normally takes a long period. Moreover, it is always much easier and less costly to sell to repeat clients rather than seeking out new clients every time.

A successful fun page has the following characteristics:

New & Interesting Content

It is bad enough to repost content derived from other fan pages. It is even worse if you repeatedly post the same content on your fan page. Many people tend to do this just so that fans that are in different time zones would have a chance to read the post. However, it is a very irritating habit and gives the impression that a fan page simply has run out of ideas.

If you must repost content, the best way to go about it is by giving it a new perspective. For instance if you posted a story of how a house disappeared into a large sink hole. A second post on the same issue could focus on the people involved in the incident. This will ensure that fans who did not get it the first time will still get the story in the second post without appearing as a repetitive post.

Fan pages that always have new and interesting content easily become top favorites for many internet users. They can also become reliable news sources for a generation that has done away with conventional news sources.

Helpful Information

Posting interesting content is not enough - giving useful information that can help your fans in daily life is even better. Such helpful information should be aligned towards your line of business. Giving helpful information to solve the real life issue of your fans is the biggest testament to your expertise. This gives potential clients more confidence in seeking your services or buying products from you.

Some fan pages are designed purely as "how to" resources. Considering that a substantial amount of organic online searches are related to "how to" issues, there will be no shortage of fans in such a page. By providing useful and effective information the fans are likely to trust the capacity of your business to deliver on its promises.

Highly Interactive

Having a large number of inactive fans is just as bad as having none at all. The comments given by fans not only create excitement within the fan page, but also provide useful feedback. This feedback will help you gauge how well your fan page is doing. The criticisms and praises from fans are vital indicators of what needs improvement in the fan page. Without such useful feedback, it is very easy for a fan page to go down the path to insignificance.

Every effort must be made to keep the fan page interactive, even if it means giving out free gifts. An interactive page will involve regular opinion polls as well as question and answer sessions. If regular posts on the page receive a substantial number of comments, it is a sure sign of how interactive the page is. Such kind of engagement makes the page fun and exciting, which attracts many more fans.

New Improvements

The online world is very dynamic and constantly changing. This is particularly so with social media where new trends and vocabularies are constantly created. If your fan page does not regularly have new improvements, it will likely become boring and less enticing to your fans.

Current online trends have seen more emphasis on infographics rather than simple text, use of images as well as videos. These are necessary additions to your Facebook posts to make them not only appealing, but current and adaptive. Many new apps are also available to make polling and opinion taking more interactive. Keeping up to date with such improvements is sure to make your fan page a success and bring in better results for your social marketing efforts.

Train Your Fans

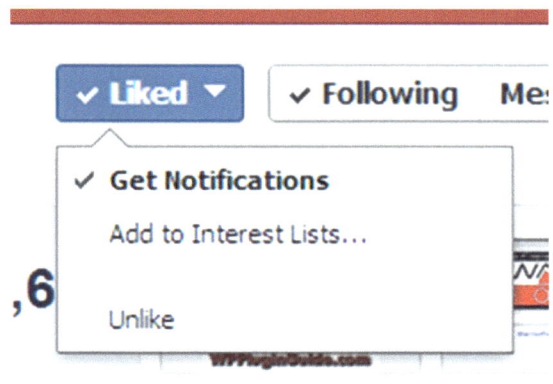

With Facebook moving toward less organic and more sponsored content going into your fans' newsfeeds - unless you show your fans how to make certain they are getting your updates - you are very likely going to find that you are only reaching 10% of your fans at any given moment.

I recommend adding a paragraph in your fan page description that explains how they should add your page to their newsfeed **using the Get Notifications item on the Liked menu.** □

BECOMING ROCK STARS

Many people consider being a rock star in their profession as a highly unlikely event, hence they don't even try. Perhaps, that is why most people never move beyond the average to exemplary one-of-a-kind success. It could be only those who are crazy enough to stick their necks out who find out that being a rock star is no impossibility.

Without trying to oversimplify the tough process of achieving rock star status on social media, there are some key aspects that are guaranteed to get you there. These aspects have continually been evident in every single person who got to the very top of their chosen profession or line of business.

Quantum Event (Big Break)

Frankly, hard work alone will rarely get you to the top, otherwise the millions of hardworking professionals who do backbreaking work daily would all be rich billionaires. Apart from the hard work that you put in to your social media presence, you need a quantum event (big break) to get to the top. This is something that will radically shift your social media efforts into prominence and get your posts going viral across multiple online platforms. The quantum event may be an affiliation with a major social media personality, a major business deal or a video upload that becomes very popular.

There is only one drawback with getting your big break: most often you cannot create it. Many times such big breaks happen all by surprise. However, there is something you can do: you can try to increase your chances of getting that big break.

You can start off by building your network of high influencers in the social media world. This can be better done through LinkedIn where many top professionals can be found. By developing close contacts with such people, you not only learn what they do to be the best, but you just might get the much needed push to the very top.

Another aspect about big breaks is that you never know where it will come from. You might assume that getting many Facebook followers will get you to the top, but it might turn out that a simple image on Instagram would be all that it takes to have a powerful impact. Hence, you need to have an open mind and also keep your eye open for opportunities to leverage on for maximum impact.

Find The Highest Impact Area

Many times we take certain things for granted simply because we do not realize their value. In fact, many people destroy their chances to get to the top simply because they cannot quantify the value of what they have. For instance many top international athletes such as the legendary Catherine Ndereba of Kenya were discouraged early in their career from "wasting" their time running. Such athletes come from poor, traditional-oriented families; whereby the girl child is expected to do more "meaningful" household chores, rather than run around "like boys". Fortunately, Catherine Ndereba realized the value in running, for which she ended up earning thousands of dollars in appearance fees, as well as handsome rewards from winning top international races.

The question to you is: *is there a part of your social media strategy that you are simply neglecting, because it simply looks meaningless and of little worth?* It might just be a regular daily chat with one of your fans. That fan might have immense influence in the social media world.

What you need to asses is both the long and short term benefits of what you do. There are obviously many day-to-day activities that are necessary for profitable running of your business, but you should not neglect the long term activities that will bring exponential results in future.

Focus On Your Best Assets

Have you ever watched a film that has so many sub-plots such that you can hardly tell what it is all about? You might even have to rewind the movie several times just to follow on the story. As for me, I would simply dump the movie at once. Unfortunately, that is exactly how many social media strategies have been implemented so far.

The marketing professionals seek to include everything and anything that is worth something, just to be on the safe side or not to miss anything important. That really frustrates Facebook fans who fail to understand what your page is all about. They would wonder whether it is a social movement, a comedy page or even a facts page.

Once you have identified your highest impact area, the simple and proven action to take is focus on it while keeping an eye out for those quantum events. When you do this for a long time, your fan page earns the reputation of offering specific information or having a specific style. This means that many people would know exactly what your fan page has to offer. It is also easier for them to refer there friends who need exactly what your fan page has to offer.

Just think of the rock stars that you know; each one has one or at most two areas by which you remember them. It can be football players, tennis stars, technology gurus or even musicians in specific genres. Likewise, when you focus your social media efforts on specific high impact areas, you will no doubt become a powerful force to reckon with.

CONCLUSION

The unique and insightful ideas presented in this book are sure to positively impact on any social media marketing strategy. However, action must be taken to implement them, otherwise they will be of little worth. Unfortunately, many people rarely implement new methods, unless forced to by circumstances (this might be something as serious as an impending business closure).

Taking into consideration this reluctance to change, you can opt to apply the various strategies given in this book alongside traditional marketing methods. Once you see the effectiveness and efficiency of the new strategies, you will have no qualms about dumping the old for the new.

One particular area that traditional marketing methods differ from the new is in advertising. Although both make use of adverts, traditional social media marketing emphasizes placing of numerous ads on social platforms, rather than engaging with the audience. This is not only costly in the long run, but does not develop the much-needed rapport with your audience, which is a great trust-builder guaranteed to turn them into paying clients.

Good social media practice not only takes into consideration the views and opinions of target audiences, but, more importantly, gets them involved in the actual implementation process. The blissfully ignorant days when clients waited for finished products without knowing how they were made or even where they came from are long gone.

With increased environmental awareness, as well as other social concerns, clients are demanding to know what you do behind the scenes. Opening up to them will not embarrass you, but instead serve to build trust and mutual understanding. In fact, the social world has a knack of finding out the juicy details of highly secretive businesses or organizations. You might as well give the truthful details rather than let some biased story leak out.

By building a strong social media presence, you will ensure your business stays in the limelight where your clients are. Whether acceptable or not, the social platform allows businesses to get into the private and intimate lives of their clients like never before. This will give you a much better understanding of the issues that truly matter to your clients. With such knowledge, you can develop customized solutions for your clients and also tap into a wide pool of prospective buyers.

ABOUT THE AUTHOR

Social media played an important role in Micheal Savoie's life in 2008 when he worked closely with Best Selling Author, Ken McArthur and his Impact Action Team to get the word out about SpeakUpSaveLives.org to help prevent teen suicides. During that period, Micheal's social media presence grew, and with it, his marketing abilities. By the end of 2008, Micheal was able to walk away from a career in retail and work for himself in online marketing. Since then, Micheal has focused on blogging and social media marketing. He hosts The Blogging With Micheal Show on Tuesdays at 11AM Eastern to discuss online marketing trends and interview some of the movers and shakers in the business. The Social Net Effect came about when he attended a marketing event in Las Vegas and found that people spent more time connecting via social media during that event than actually listening to the speakers. Social media marketing quickly became his favorite way to help clients grow their presence online. Micheal now uses social media marketing as a way to grow his listener base for his podcast and the readership for his blogs.

Want more social media marketing information? I have a Social Net Effect Fan Page on Facebook where I will keep you up to date with videos and articles about one or more of the social networks and how people are using them to further their social media marketing.

Just head over to Facebook.com/SocialNetEffect and click LIKE!

BONUS

Thank You For Purchasing This Book!

As a bonus for purchasing this book, you can download this free resource guide chock full of tools that social media marketers are using to get the word out about their product or service. I will also keep you updated on the latest social media marketing trends, software, tricks and tips. Just fill out the short survey, and I'll send you the guide!

SocialNetEffect.com/resourceguide

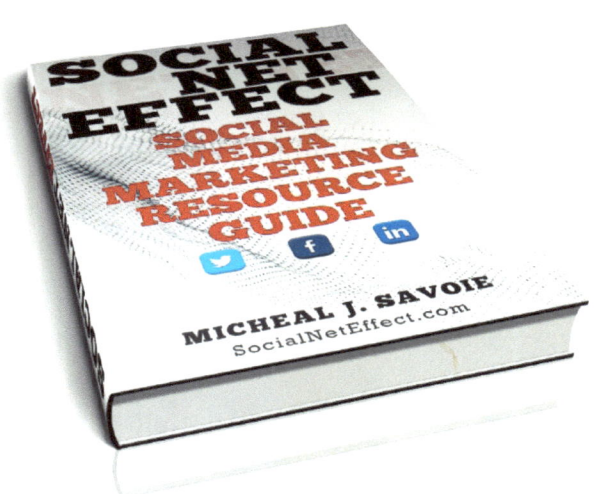

I need your help!

To keep making Social Net Effect better and to create even more amazing new books in this series, I would appreciate it if you would leave an honest review of this book on Amazon! By leaving a review, you are helping me come up with new topics and making my books even better. Please head over to Amazon and leave a review using the following URL:

SocialNetEffect.com/fishingforprospects